Red Door Blue Frame

Red Door Blue Frame

EMELINE GLOVER

RESOURCE *Publications* • Eugene, Oregon

RED DOOR BLUE FRAME

Resource Publications
An Imprint of Wipf and Stock Publishers
199 W. 8th Ave., Suite 3
Eugene, OR 97401

www.wipfandstock.com

PAPERBACK ISBN: 979-8-3852-0082-5
HARDCOVER ISBN: 979-8-3852-0083-2
EBOOK ISBN: 979-8-3852-0084-9

02/27/24

For the suitcase I came from.
And the loved ones who helped me grow out of it.

this collection of writing contains themes and descriptions of events that may be difficult and/or potentially triggering for some individuals. please take the time for yourself before, during, and after reading.

Contents

if you ask me to describe to you, the plaster and the boards, the rooms and all their doors, that make me, i will tell you instead, of treetops and forest floor. of tadpoles and snapping turtles lazy in the creek. of fireflies and june bugs. of bike rides and dirt roads and hand clapping games. i will not tell you of the red door, nor the blue frame. of the cracking sun-burned paint peeling off the wood and siding. of the first floor or the second. nor will I walk the stairs with you, hands on the rail exposing each indent and skid mark, showing you where the carpet has thinned and started to unravel. instead i will lead you up the gravel path to the town limits where a bridge dwarfs a crick dragging itself towards the river, to the twig fence two little hands labored over, to the garden a daisy-colored girl scarred the earth for, raking sand and gravel together in neat lines broken up by wilting petunias and lilacs. and I will leave you there and hope you understand. i will hope you understand.

little garden girl with the black thumb

as a child i was a jealous gardener
fingernails stained and caked with red earth
stealing marigolds and crab apple blossoms
from picket fenced yards
stashing them in a rusted-out tomato soup can
filled with grimy rainwater that would slosh over
the front spokes of my bicycle as i rode
down to turkey creek five miles out of town
to a bridge that covered a trickle of mountain
shed water and my hideaway in the woods

here
i was a collector of dead things

planting and planting
but inevitably the wilting stems
would slump forward succumbing
to ambivalent nature
and i would come racing back with hope
that something was alive

i didn't understand the lesson

we do not grow without roots

second is the first to lose

my father was a car enthusiast/car junky/would spend more than what he earned on a project/despite the empty fridge at home/a reckless kind of collector/there was nothing in the world that he loved more than a 9-second car screaming down a mile track/and he named me after his favorite model/bought a baby blue sleeper GT to mark my arrival in the world/his buddy at the track, i wore my baseball cap backwards to fit in with the boys/shared his love for the rumble and the smell of burning rubber/of dirt tracks, motor way walking tacos and cajun style ribs around tire rim fire pits/ he thrived at the track/with the guys, in the dirt and grime/no wife in sight/i was supposed to be his little dude, his wing-man/

my father named me after his favorite car/

what good is a second best

holy/intention

my mother spoon fed us
the writings of john when empty bellies
cried too loudly,
built walls out of the gospels,
as the house crumbled around her,
walked children through a marriage
blessed at the wrong altar,
[michael only means *like* god]
reciting the lessons taught to the disciples,
hoping they would make a difference.
she married a man too like david
and watched him fall just the same.
too caught up in the spectacle
to walk away.

psalm 2: a man like david

how else are you to react
when you see a dead man walking
than to gather his bones
into your body and say
rest here.

stay

in a place of waiting, where you must pull and push and yet nothing breaks. moves. gives. the doors seem to hold themselves shut. the windows unsettled in their frames. the cabinets open ever so slightly. the house is holding her breath. i am held here. in this home. this space. we let your emptiness reverberate around this vacant dwelling place. all I hear. stay. stay. stay.

[unnamed]

we.

newspaper crown queens with scepters of scrawny tree limb
marching and roaring our seven-year-old truth to ruthless sky
and molly grass meadow.
screaming and dancing and howling to the whispered promise of
mother nature.

we.

are of wild breeding.

we.

daughters of imagination, had no concept of frailty in this sum-
mer haze. we were only of what the forest was. only comprised of
burning light beams and the cracked log bark of fallen trees. we
rose and set with the sun and rejoiced in her return each morn-
ing. her pink-blush smile beckoning us to come out and play.
our sunshine-speckled backs would be red from her intense gaze
as we twisted and shouted, gleeful in grass-stained shorts and
tees.

we.

joyful in the glimpses of summer, free from parental oppres-
sion until night fall, would spend solstice hours far away from
"house not home." splashing and racing through pine and river.
our games as wild as the hair atop our heads. our despair at her
departure would echo against her blue-black shawl as the light-
post in the center of town would cough and wheeze at the sight
of the moon's sad crescent expression. our crowns hanging low
and sneakers scuffing as we mourned in funeral procession what
nighttime meant. our knightly shadows from daytime no longer
standing guard over our shoulder, we marched side by side to the
red front door.

. . ..

we.

in her august gaze, grew like weeds,
unobservant of the passing summer days leading into changing
leaves and colder times.

man and daisy paper

man swings hammer at daisy-colored wall, sending plumes of ancient dust up into the air, dancing in arcs of light, lazily shifting between the shafts. in a quiet hour after wall has come down, layers of grime cover tarps and materials, blanketing the skeleton of this house. bones of wood smelling like change and indifference, they stand strong against the continued destruction.

man swings fist and foot at daisy-colored girl, sending petal-white hair into the air, ripping and pulling, it dances in the light, lazily falling amidst the onslaught. in a quiet hour after man has calmed, daisy girl is covered in grime, sits amongst the wrecked skeleton of this house, her clothes smelling of sweat and salt: change and indifference, she stands small against the continued destruction.

"we're moving"

i didn't think that meant this house would burn.

9

remember a time when
we couldn't stand to be
in the same room
without screaming the
walls apart/remember
the nights we circled
our despair and called
it rage, shoving it in
boxes throwing that
pain together/we sent it
to the attics in
ourselves saying we'll
sort it out another day/
we let it fester in the
dust and heat, dim
lighting making us
forgetful/remember
the heaviness that sat
with us, tiring and
stagnant/remember a
weight that wasn't ours
to share.

snow dancers

i will never forget the way your wind-chapped cheeks glowed glee-
ful in the winter sun, bright against your florescent green coat. you
were small amongst the grey trees, bare and lonely and bending
under the piles of snow. we played for hours in the woods, watch-
ful of where you meandered until we weren't. your green coat no
longer so noticeable, you were simply gone.

i remember standing there, watching the snow erupt in motion as
we realized you were no longer with us. small and fragile snow-
flakes caught up in a frenzy of panic. the wind catching them and
taking them every which way. in that moment, the winter air didn't
seem to care that you were missing, it simply carried the snow
from one place to another.

you were found just a few minutes later, lying against a snowbank,
a tiny green mountain dusted in white, too tired to move from
your day of play—you had decided a nap had been in order.

your feet scuffed the snow on the way home, kicking up more
snowflakes into the air. they twisted around you as you scowled at
the road, hearing over and over again the dangers of being too cold
and falling asleep in the snow.

years later we watched a layer of snow cover the remains of our
charred and twisted home and you turned to me, flakes frozen
on your eyelashes and cheeks, and you said it felt like that day so
many years ago, like falling asleep in the snow.

i have tasted dust in my memories

we watched your taillights burn to dust/red eyes in the night miraged in a smoky haze/until the only sound was the nighttime and raindrops hitting dead grass and gravel/it wasn't raining/but i think the sky was weeping/or it was me/or you/i do not pretend to know the inner workings of a man who drove off and left two children in the middle of a dirt road with a busted up suitcase and a 'behave'/i remember being ushered into bed late that night/or maybe it was morning/and frantic phone calls/hushed whispers/a never ending stream of 'this will be alright'/or 'he'll come back'/ spoiler/you didn't come back and you didn't call/MIA/a father of the year photo frame from three years back took up space in my brain and the suitcase/we were told you would come back in a week/you would come back/ come back

nuclear

i had a small elementary class of twelve students, mostly girls,
and a homeroom teacher just out of college. she was a nervous
woman, and i don't remember many of her lessons.
but she taught me addition and subtraction.

mother + father + two children = nuclear (normal)

the atom bomb being my family just didn't add up

polite dinner conversation

"you can hate me if you want to."

a statement i wasn't expecting to come from you, my mind was already made up regarding our relationship—a junk drawer of memories, a filing cabinet labeled: mother—do not open.

but the silence punctuated by the 'snick' of the front door closing as i entered your home told me more than the vague and stuttering phone call prompting me to come to town ever would.

you were hiding for the first time in my life at the back of the house, surrounding yourself in the aromas of a time when i still clung to your side, begging to belong.

"you can hate me if you want to."

you brandish the mixing bowl and wooden spoon, filling up the silence with a rhythmic scraping instead of an explanation. it had been years since you asked me what my favorite meal was but tonight you decided whatever you had to tell me would be easier to digest with memories of home cooked meals to wash it down.

"he's not your dad.
we used to joke about it.
but he's not your dad."

you continued stirring.

my mother prays every night

surely this   will kill you.
she takes my hand and she clings,
skin to skin, bone to bone
but i am foreign matter to her dna
and she does not understand the indifference in me
is unavoidable.
i don't tell her that i am already dying, made promises to the earth
to let this body decay in the solemn silence of youth, to grow wild-
flowers from my brain matter.

i want to lie still for a moment and not feel the waves of my regret
pull my feet into the ocean of my guilt. my inability to exist cor-
rectly. i want to exhale and never have to worry if my breathing is
tolerable. i want to tell her of all the times that i wished to slip into
the wilderness and let the continuous ebbing consume me. let it
overcome me.

my mother holds me once again as i disintegrate between her
palms. she does not have the melancholy months and years of
hearing infants' night-time screaming to prepare her for my salt-
crusted pleas, but her bargaining is still the same. begging for a
night of rest, her eyes are heavy with an unnamed grief.

she repeats herself. like a mantra. holding me to this place.

june first

the ending of april usually brought invitations to grad parties, barbeques, pool parties. we'd find them littered among the rolls of bubble wrap and packing tape, used as scratch paper—to write down where each box was going, what still needed to be packed. like clockwork, they would appear on the dining room table signaling the end of our time at that house—we moved every year—for six years—on june first, all in one day. from july to march those houses would begin to take shape, would start to feel like home, only to be condensed back into boxes and packed up again. after a few years you learn to never unpack, always ready to go out the door, you keep the memories in shrink wrap and learn to let go of the idea of having a space that's all your own. learn to compartmentalize what you need, what you don't. we would never be the kind of family with stenciled in heights, the crayon drawings that never quite came off. my mother would tell us that's the sacrifice we made. what was never built, never broke—she'd say you can't lose what you never made.

to-do

i collect my dishes placing them in the correct sink
and sweep the linoleum and lean against the wall while
i brush my teeth staring at the floorboards and
i walk the dog and choke down my
food and i organize my self-help books along
the wall in clear view so that when i eventually
extend the invitation people notice that i'm
getting better and i brush my hair and i drive a bit
slower and i keep my fingernails clean and i keep
doing all of these things like check marks in a catalogue
and i'm waiting to get better. i want to get better.

for a moment i thought there was a god

last night i dreamt of your funeral/there were no women at the foot of your grave/no brothers in arms to shoulder the burden of your life in its final procession/no weeping or wailing or gnashing of teeth/i watched as you struck at the void holding you in between time and space/looking for someone to blame or coax into taking your place/on your face i saw every blow you ever dealt/it wrecked your skin/your blue eyes sunken and dead/twisted you into familiar shapes of rage and desperation/you kept screaming but nothing came about/your string had already been cut/the death bell already set tolling/the fields surrounding my childhood home sprung around you/dragging you down further to your knees/wrapping you in dead weeds/they continued to twist and shift/masking you into their green and yellow/ consuming you and i forgot your voice as you faded/in your place wildflowers started to push through/careful and small/their fragile heads held higher and higher as they grew/a reminder to live and grow/

to continue

i awoke to flowers on my nightstand/and i thought of you/and for the first time in a long time/i did not die with your memory/

perhaps i am growing too

pushing daisies

i am not a ghost or a shadow stuck to the wall of this house but i drift here from room to room grasping at the relics of a girl who is me and who is not me, learning a history i wrote on my bones and covered with layers of daisies.

my mother calls me pretty/a blue eyed blonde hair replica of america's dying dream/daisy without her gatsby/a porcelain girl with too much of an interest in the mechanics of bowling balls in china shops/she calls me pretty/as if it was the key/to the front gate/or a room/or her own concept of chains/motherhood she names it/ five girls/twenty-eight years old/her youth was chewed up and spit out of five hungry mouths/but she calls us her miracles/we who taught her more than life itself/she says she wouldn't trade it/but jokes that we stole her best years to split amongst ourselves/she calls me pretty/when i tell her i want to take the harder road/want to choose a different path/she stops me and calls me pretty/and says that i could enter any room i please if i only had the man to guide me/to open up the door/as long as i didn't glance too long at the reflection in the glass ceiling/i would be happy/ but she calls me pretty/and i have to wonder if that means she's not/ we look so different her and i/brown hair brown eyes/no college degree/ marriage number three/gave up everything just to leave his house alive/left behind her vanity/a chest of drawers/her dignity/her wedding ring/and apparently she deserved it because she's not like me/not pretty/not pretty/not pretty/not worthy of a person who loved her unconditionally/despite the wrinkles in her story/and the scars and lessons learned a bit too early/she calls me pretty/and i want to know why she isn't/deserving/of pretty

remember the crying, the
healing of it all/remember you
held me tightly when I was
small: porcelain girl in a very
scary world/remember the days
spent lazy and
laughing/remember the fear of
emergency room visits and
worried crying/the times you
spent awake, exhausted but
steadfast next to us/remember
fevers and chicken pox and pink
eye/remember how you loved
before he broke our home.

5, 6, 7, 8

i learned to sing hand clapping rhymes in the back of a yellow
school bus on the thirty-minute drive to the elementary building,
learned miss mary mack had black buttons all up and down her
back and that boys go to jupiter to get more stupider and you could
sit with the older girls as long as you didn't complain when your
hands started hurting.

i saw my sisters for the first time in over two years and instead of
exchanging the typical small talk and awkward silences, we played
handclapping games until we were a tangle of laughing girls again,
only caring about the rhythm and the nursery rhymes. ignoring
the pain in our palms to hold onto the little children we never got
to be.

a ghost story

... and i can remember a girl who stood at the
window looking to the blues and greens and spotty
dreams of the horizon and questioned whether the
hills in the distance were the mountains in her
textbooks and if she lived in a bowl of trees. she was
dust caught in the front porch stair well, her hand
carding through light beams believing it to be a
million tiny organisms and not just the air and dust
she breathed.   she is still there,
                                                     drifting

when you tell someone you
want to die, their eyes widen ever
so slightly and they rush about
to try and save the image of
you in their head

but i tell you i want to die
and you glance at me with
eyes like mine
and you sigh into the silence

and i know
you feel the stone in your chest
grinding your bones a bit each day
the weight stopping up your lungs
sealing away your voice
until it's an echo in an elegy
in your mothers keening

and suddenly i am not alone
in this world

and i am terrified

brown bear

I.

i am sitting in the church pew where you taught me to read music/center column, three pews back, slightly to the right of being centered/"the music is pretty right here"/you could never seem to find the right pitch/but the look on your face when the organ played was reason enough to sing along as loudly as i could.

II.

my 13th birthday you sat on the porch/beaming/i was unwrapping a gift you had grandma help you with/paper and tape were never things you got along with/you were so excited you ruined the surprise.

III.

i cried when you told me that in order to go fishing i had to put the worm on by myself/"yur a big girl. worms don't bite do they?"/ we compromised/i got gummy worms for a snack/you baited my hook when it was time.

IV.

you are seated at the back of the church/your chair is one that was hand carved and lined with velvet/you are wearing your easter best even though it is mid-february/your face is waxen and a perfect replica/but it is not you.

V.

my thoughts halt as the pastor begins the service/your brothers
and friends carry you up the aisle and lay you center/your face
lights up on the wall/i am watching years/you/pulling us on the
three-wheeler/our cheeks are bright pink and our smiles are lost
in our hand-me-down hats/you/in the swimming pool/tossing us
in the air so that we might make a cannonball splash as impressive
as yours/you/holding the lead to "spice"/waving and laughing even
as i looked on terrified/you/sitting at the breakfast table explain-
ing that cheerios/frosted flakes/*and* wheaties/are in fact best when
combined/you/playing hide-and-go-seek in the barn/even though
you were always it.

VI.

as i entered the church and saw you/i got the feeling that i could
simply lay my hand on your shoulder/that the gentle pressure of
my fingers would be enough of a plea/you would wake up/like
early sunday mornings/and we would sing the church hymns.

VII.

the service is ending/the choir is singing your favorite hymn/it is
joyless and sorrowful/so unlike the merriment it brought you on
easter sunday/i am still waiting for you to walk in/to ask about the
crops/the weather/the neighbor boys/but you lay peaceful, finally
at your long-awaited home/and for a moment/ "the music is pretty
right here."

apricity

there is sunshine

eyelash thin and so pale upon the earth, a shivering grey
surrounded by snowflake upon snowflake

seeping into crevices between concrete and pebble under foot

i want to catch the liquid spell holding silent daybreak together

if i could give you this morning to show you i'm trying i would
scrape it off the sidewalk and present it to you like a clump of daf-
fodils picked thoughtfully off the playground but the daybreak
would still only say to you what it says to me.

we will have to start again this day. we will have to start again.

there is pleading

tonight shapeless and heartless echoing out into the yard

dead dog

dead dog

is it not enough that i have tried to be good

consumption

starvation is a companion borne to me
so you see,
i have always known hunger.
been a bit more wolf rather than red
i skipped the petal eyelashes and baby soft hair
and grew my own kind of skin.
put the witch's brew under my tongue
instead of candy liqueur
- they call me acidic
and say that i'm cold and i'm wild
but my gut turned to stone to survive
on empty promises and pretty words
so i do not mind
when they ask
where the girl with the tendency
to stray into fields of flowers
has gone.

tell them to call off the huntsmen,
to put down the hatchet and the axe.

there is no girl here.

~~my mother~~ prays ~~every night~~

surely this~~, will kill you.~~
~~she takes~~ my ~~hand and she clings,~~
skin ~~to skin, bone to~~ bone
~~but I am foreign matter to her~~ dna
~~and she does not understand the indifference in me.~~
~~is unavoidable.~~
~~i don't tell her that i am already~~ dying~~, made promises to the earth~~
~~to let this body decay in the solemn silence of youth, to grow wild~~
~~flowers from my brain matter.~~

i ~~want to~~ lie still ~~for a moment and not feel the waves of my regret~~
~~pull my feet into the ocean of my guilt. my inability to~~ exist ~~cor-~~
~~rectly. i want to~~ exhale ~~and never have to worry if my breathing is~~
~~tolerable. i want to tell her of all the times that i wished to slip into~~
~~the wilderness and let the continuous ebbing consume me. let it~~
~~overcome me.~~

~~my mother holds me as once again as i~~ disintegrate ~~between her~~
~~palms. she does not have the melancholy months and years of~~
~~hearing infants' night-time screaming to prepare her for my salt-~~
~~crusted pleas, but her bargaining is still the same. begging for a~~
~~night of rest, her eyes are heavy with an unnamed grief.~~

~~she repeats herself. like a mantra. holding me to this place.~~

i placed my hand on a burning kettle once and came away blistered and angry and i tried to tell you of what it must mean but you told me not everything has to mean something, someday i will have to stop becoming the things that happen to me

gravity

there was a time i thought you fixed it, celebrating another birth-
day, another year gone by. out in the front yard with the sun sinking
low in the ditch, i must have been seven or perhaps eight but you
two were young again, for that wonderful year, laying side by side
too far off to hear the words exchanged between you. the year we
got the trampoline was probably the best one i can remember be-
cause you'd run out the door on a saturday afternoon shouting for
us to go back inside or to go off on a bike ride, because it was your
"only grown-ups" time. and you'd lay on the cold nylon and point
up at the clouds or you'd roll around laughing until that sound was
all that we heard from you and i don't know what you talked about
but you fought less and smiled more and for one whole year we all
thought it was all going to get better. i couldn't miss the trampoline
more

are you not to pity a man
so burdened that he has turned
himself inside out and
lost the humanity that
makes him whole.

remember where we
started/now look at
where we are/unpacking
the boxes in that attic
and letting go/scraping
off the dust and airing
out the spaces he carved
himself into/see how
the light floods this
house/see how we've
remodeled/see how we
survived/

we survived.

i read somewhere that when spoken to kindly and with words of praise, plants grow healthier and with much more viscosity than plants spoken to harshly so if i am to cut off this family tree and grow a sapling from new roots, i might first apologize for mistaking overflowing with plenty. i have not learned the difference between flooding and just enough. drowning and drought. and i have killed plenty a plant in my time but i am trying to change this black thumb of mine into a hand that is gentle. a hand that is kind. not just to others but to myself. most importunately myself. so i will keep replanting until roots too strong to pull and leaves too high to reach cover me and hold me steadfast. and i will grow in this garden i have planted. and it will be enough. i will be enough.

first of june

my mother was so excited to show off the new house—a burnt
sienna orange optical illusion trick with 'enough rooms to house a
circus' and weren't we the circus. she proudly exclaimed that this
would be the first june in six years we didn't have to wonder where
we would be in twelve months' time—this was our house. our
home. so they painted just about every square inch of it and even
bought a house plant. they replaced flooring and lighting fixtures,
repaired walls, finished the garage. and if you looked close enough
you could see it was almost enough to repair the foundation of
their marriage when they redid the back porch and garden. but
when june first came, the house was empty. she had packed up—
moved on, finally fed up with his unpacked baggage. he sold the
house, we moved again. and waited for another first june where we
knew where we were going.

the   dreaming   turns   to   d r i f t i n g

into the
left
lane as a misfiring of chemicals draws the conclusion that my
                car would look better   in the
                                        newspaper,
a crumpled picture next to my obituary,   title: a
tragedy.

                                        my life
spread open   [but fabricated]   to eulogize   [and   cover
up]
the ugly truth: after everything life handed to me and after
everything i managed to carry, my biggest goal was to always
drop it all and

                                        disappear.

i'd spend my mornings fantasizing, sitting in the window facing
the forests and willing myself to walk out the door. always hoping
to slip into the green and grey surrounding the house and sit in the
quiet hysteria that permeated the walls and seemed to dwell there.

i think it's why my favorite color is green; it lacks any sort of as-
sociation other than my mornings sitting and watching the trees
and thinking to myself, 'i'm going to bury myself under a canopy
of juniper and evergreen.'

but the split second when my car lurches is gone and the trees fade
back in the recesses of my mind. their green rattling through my
skull as my eyes focus on the road and my mind begins to yet again
                                        d r i f t

ticking time bomb

we trade small pleasantries
and call them our griefs
dress them up
and bestow them silly little names—
"i'm simply tired, i haven't been sleeping"

evading the choking
iron around our necks
dogs in the backyard
starving
waiting for a link to break

what is a lighthouse to a seabird

i became a shadow the day i tumbled through my first fragile
footsteps, chasing after you as you stalked through
fatherhood, wanting to be just like you but always falling so
far behind. so i morphed into shapes, shifting myself in an
attempt to match your gait. first a shadow, then a nuisance,
never just a child but i didn't know any other way.

yet, i wonder if perhaps i was more a bird circling a
lighthouse. you were architecture beyond my own language
and i never knew what to call you—a monolith out amongst
the sea, dominating any horizon i found myself in.

i do not know if we remember all the good times—the
summer days on the trampolines, or the smell of pine and
flashes of sunlight between nettles, but i remember revolving
around you, so foreign in the landscape of my childhood and
yet i tried to name you father, to build myself a home in biting
stone.

but how does a seabird name a lighthouse

how does a seabird go home

you asked me how it happened/simple/point blank/recognizing the empty shotgun shell demeanor upon my arrival/but you were still wearing kevlar/a yellow notepad/blue ink/separating the action from emotion/and i would use the window to glance the cars outside/timing my responses with the shifting of gravel under tires/one clue for every drive by/you asked me how it happened/i'd mumble/that's a lot of years to talk about/you'd smile and say we've got time/pen poised/armor raised/i made you cry that day/ because i told you i never quite grew out of panicking in the night/ how walking into a darkened room still felt like the closet door closing behind me/i stumbled through the part where i mentioned two weeks/you'd asked how long/ and i had committed the furniture grain to memory/hoping maybe the couch was the only one who heard me/but i told you/i told you what he did/how he locked me in that room for two weeks and let me scream/crying i was sorry for something i didn't understand/and then you asked me how i lived/and i said i hadn't/i had played hangman/guessing at the password that would finally let me out/but i had run out rope/instead ripping the binding off a mattress/if i was to lose it wouldn't be because i wasn't resourceful/you had stopped writing by this point/my sarcasm no longer deflecting/and suddenly i felt full of gunpowder again/admitting/i wish i hadn't made it/finally able to say it out loud/you looked at me and sighed/and the room was silent/and you cried for me/and with me/and i knew/i knew that you felt that feeling too/and it terrified me/to think the person who was supposed to be helping me felt like me/but you smiled/a small and watery thing/and you apologized for the child that had died that day in the closet/asking if i grieved her/i hadn't understood what you meant that day/now eight years passed/but now/ as i listen to my friends/my family/what i see are their cemeteries/ hidden beneath their clothes/masked behind pensive stares/and i wondered who mourns them/as you mourned for me that day/all the unnamed children they've left behind/the griefs and trials and devastations we bury deep within ourselves/who weeps for them/ remembers their purpose/were their deaths and our deaths all in vain/chalked up to a cruel existence/the unfairness of it all that allows us to get up and walk away/forgetting and rotting/i remember i once asked why must i dredge the past back up/regurgitating the sour memories for analysis/and you said because they fester/all the unmarked graves we've dug/but if you go back and visit them/ and take care of them/keep the gravestones clean/the grass trim/ the flowers fresh/the cemetery becomes peaceful/and it doesn't hurt so much to go there/i had stared at you as i often did/brows pulled forward in a scowl/contemplating/i didn't believe you/as children never do/but i began tidying up my graveyard this year/ starting with the oldest sites/writing down their names and their details/honoring their life/or lack thereof/and it isn't quite peaceful/but it isn't quite so painful/and i think i understand now/all the graves we've made into ourselves/we're all just a collection of walking cemeteries/praying that someone will see our headstones and read our griefs and stay and mourn awhile/and when they leave/ the site will be a little better/a little brighter/and the pain won't visit as much/so now i try to walk around with daisy seeds/clenched against my palm/scattering them as i visit with others/myself/ hoping the tears will water the flowers and help grow something beautiful/and perhaps others will see me and wonder at what i am doing/but maybe /they'll find their own seeds/and scatter them around/and those plants will grow/ and a little peace will be found

first june

i repainted the living room three times before i settled for a shade of green one could argue i had painted the walls with the first time around. i rearranged furniture monthly until slowly the pieces clicked into place and i was religious in showcasing the various holidays around the house. i hung up paintings and photos and art i'd been gifted, placed plants around the house until they dominated most of the space. i refinished the bathroom, the kitchen, and replaced two ceiling fans (well my dad did but i supervised) getting rid of the dust caked monstrosities from the eighties. i planted a vegetable garden and fixed up the fireplace and my friends came over often and when the first of june came around i didn't notice. there were no boxes left packed in the closet, knick-knacks closed up in safe keeping for someday. i had made myself a space all my own and for the first time, june was simply june.

mothers day

are you only
a part of me and in my way
profoundly the mover of my life /
not an inheritance of skin color
of bone structure of hair texture
but of grieving and mourning /
existing in the gentleness
of morning toast and eggs
or in the desperate grasping breath
of the twilight hours where phantoms
remind us of all that we were never given /
could i see in you the same
maternity i see in others
and if so would you see
in me the gift of childhood

this body is a coffin

i hold an elegy in my palms/cradled and shaded from view /
mourning amidst the graves/that i am/a child laid low in sand and
soil/buried over/over/over/a grief i clutch between my fingers/i
try to hold them/as they should have been held/but i cannot hold
myself/and so i let the prayer clasped between my ribs/thudding
up through my stomach/settle in my breast bone/carve an entreaty
into my sternum/so that it might become me/ and i try to unfurl
my hand/to share the weight i've held/white knuckled/to plant
seeds amongst graves/to remind myself/i did not die here/i live/i
live/i live

daisy girl

the dying stems and leaves under the bridge will only ever drown
and rot. they will not grow—despite your best efforts and all your
well wishes—a plant without roots can only decay, and those sto-
len stems and flowers will not bloom into the gardens outside the
homes you stop and stare into.

put down the spade. grow your roots daisy girl.

grow your roots.

there's an expanse of grass where the front porch once stood and the tree stump we climbed and lept from is stripped of its bark and blackened. the lilac bushes we planted one summer are in various states of dying or rotting and they form a crooked fence going up the drive, as if the house was playing hide and seek behind them. that is, if there was much of the house left to play. now it is simply a pile of smoldering wood surrounded by fire marshals, reflecting the flashing lights back out into the darkening forest. the sunset appears to light the house back up again and we couldn't tell if it was still burning. but the red door and blue frame stood upright somehow. there was no kitchen to walk into, no living room floor to slide across. the second story had been brought down into the basement in most places even though the staircase remained where it was. but the front door with our height marks etched into the blue frame stood scorched but upright. and i remember finding it comical that the fire chief opened it up instead of stepping around when we were finally allowed to go inside to see the extent of the damage, as if he was welcoming us in and we had simply been gone somewhere instead. but there was nothing to come back to now and i remember how much my mother cried. we were told much later how my father had lit the fire himself, dug a hole in the foundation and ignited the insolation because my mother was going to leave him and he could think of nothing else but destroying the one thing she owned without him. and children don't know how to name their grief but i think we buried him there in the midst of his own destruction, a father, a husband. years later we went back after the rubble had been removed and the lot emptied. we had taken the red door and placed it at the opening of our childhood tree fort, not willing to part with it. and the grass had grown up around it and the trees held it steadfast and when we opened the door, everything was exactly how we had left it and time seemed to have forgotten us. and i'd like to think that somewhere, four little girls are running around in the sunshine, grass stains on their knees and smiles on their faces and all you hear is laughing and everything's okay. it's okay.

www.ingramcontent.com/pod-product-compliance
Lightning Source LLC
Chambersburg PA
CBHW071740020426
42331CB00008B/2103